Also by Nicholas A. Price

Poetry Books

AN ELEPHANT IN MY FRONT YARD: *AND OTHER OBSERVATIONS*

FORGOTTEN HOLIDAY: *AND OTHER POEMS*

BRIDGES TO MANHATTAN: *AND OTHER POETIC JOURNEYS*

Fine Art Photography Books

CLEARED HOT!

PLAYGROUND OF THE GODS

HISTORIC ICONS

For Gracie and Pinky

THOUGHTS OF YOU
and other love poems

by

Nicholas A. Price

A Tough Tribe Book

THOUGHTS OF YOU: *AND OTHER LOVE POEMS*
A Tough Tribe Book
Copyright © 2011 Nicholas A. Price

Cover design by S. J. Harris

Cover images and internal illustrations courtesy of Nicholas A. Price ©
2005-2010. All rights reserved

Library of Congress Catalogue in Publication Data on file with the
publisher

First Edition
ISBN 13: 978-0-9798390-3-0
Produced in NEW YORK
Printed and published in the USA
www.ToughTribe.com

OPM 10 9 8 7 6 5 4 3 2 1

THOUGHTS OF YOU

Alone with my cranium in the clouds,
Away from the restrictive roof of grounded burden,
Floating among the soft white cotton,
Meddling with every strand,
Invigorated by those thoughts of you,
A downpour hammering,
On an experienced rusty tin roof,
Catching fleeting shelter beneath,
Throbbing fingers frozen, a mass of degrees below,
Home again, indulging in combined warmth,
A day of rushing, desecration of time,
Cleansing water and your slender hands,
Paced out dehydrating miles, soul searching hot sun,
Clear crystal torrents, liquid diamonds on our lips,
A deliberating jury, upon my shoulders again,
Discovering your warmth on those cool clean sheets,
Foot to the floor, wheeled hands,
Tedious skirmishing drivers,
Reaching the coast,
Strolling barefoot through the breakers,
Joining the weather, falling to earth again,
With a clear head and thoughts of you.

A SIMPLE LOVE

When you are absent I lament,
Glancing at the blank pillow neighboring mine,
Indented by a spiraling night,
Printed with perplexing dreams,
Searching an atmosphere,
Infused with passing perfume,
Symbolic scent, a promised homecoming,
Stirring to disorder, a dizzy departure,
Draped fashion decisions, corresponding smalls,
Skewed mirror and brush, combed long black hair,
An artist's palette of curious things,
Powders and pastes, highlighted hues,
Partly closed drawers, half finished tea,
A simple white cup imprinted, red lipstick, full lips,
Breadcrumbs and thoroughly torched toast,
A time telling tepid kettle, plated crusts,
Photographs remain on restrictive walls,
Holding my thoughts,
A single dimensional tale,
Smiling towards a vacant void,
Sufficing until I see you in the flesh.

BRANDED

Her lustrous eyes stroked me with a lava brush,
Painting a burning memory on my humble soul,
A cruel weekend artist, with no consequential regard,
She would leave me hanging, somewhere unframed,
Slightly leaning to the side, never perfectly level,
An attic or cellar space,
A rarely used hallway bathroom,
Reserved for visiting tradesmen and passersby,
Probably with the seat always up, no female callers,
Never displayed in the great receiving room,
Banqueting guests and ceremonial gossip,
Salacious tales of daily conquests and branded hearts.

INNOCENCE

You had occupied my heart for so long,
Four corridors along,
Well after the numerous boxes
of daily sleeve romances,
Someplace on the left hand side,
Third filing cabinet, second drawer down,
Eight manila folders in,
Way ahead of those preceding loves,
Broken hearts, forgotten songs,
The earliest memories, somewhere in my head,
On a cluttered cerebral desk,
Buried in the depths of scribbled dissertations,
Orderly some days, with so much to accomplish,
Those partial projects and greater plans,
Achievements eclipsed by unpaid bills,
Tapered horizons, sustaining nameless towns,
Spacious vistas and distant seas,
Proliferating planets, liberated spirits,
One afternoon I will archive the rest,
Hoarding just you, in my innocent library.

MATADORESS

Glossy black tresses, plainly scraped,
Drum taut, against your strong-minded head,
Chiseled perfection, clear countenance,
Not an ounce of your stark beauty obscured,
Merely a humble hint of warrior rouge,
Toying with a faultless complexion,

The gutturally gruesome horde hollers,
The vivacious silk of your dress,
Bringing them to attentive adulation,
Shimmering with ravishing radiance,
The intrepid shroud of a ruthless torero,

Black, red, gold; Negra, rojo, oro,

Challenged hardheartedly,
A simple sacrificial bull,
Upon a quest for absolution,
Craving your zealous affection,

Negra, your smoldering eyes consume,
Rojo, your blood hungry impulses,
Oro, your mirrored captivating cape,

Obsession brings a merciless aggressor,

Black mesmeric eyes, calm and cruel
Red thrown frail fabric, your disguise,
Gold silk manifesting, callous steel,

Soon within the formidable clutches,
The rigid embrace of the Matadoress.

BROKEN HEART

We broke our hearts for the last time,
I stooped, picking up the crushed remains,
Searching the warped worn floorboards,
Occasionally, looking up at a dark space left wanting,
She crammed her smile, into the bottom drawer,
With the memories of us,
Crumpled receipts, faded photos,
Ribbons and dried boxed flowers,
Wedding garters, first date travel,
Paris and Rome forgotten,
Time rode a charging horse,
Sprinting into the distance of once fresh hope,
Leaving us with a sky stacked pile,
History and red tape numbers,
Rivers of undrinkable tears,
An isolated trampled landscape,
I left the heart pieces there,
Searching for seeds, ready to plant anew,
Watering and nurturing, love remaining,
Healing troubled hearts, judging her yielding lips,
Rummaging through the weary dresser for her smile,
Planting it once again, on the face of my best friend.

DANDELION CLOCKS

Time floated past on dandelion clocks,
A fragile balance between the two of us,
Embraced by ironwood ties,
Flattened by the thundering Rex,
Grumbling resonance filing at our brittle bones,
Upon a governed expedition,
Trekking around the sun,
Passing through resting pastures,
Sighting the sea and matchstick bathers,
Drawn to the evenly engraved panorama,
Quarrelling with storms and downy days,
Marching with a clattering pulse,
Shifting to the earth of humble feet,
Rolling with the chime of stationary clocks,
Obstruction pressed to the margin,
Flighty seeds pinched into the apathetic air,
A chance to start again.

SPRING

I had nearly forgotten her,
Until she arrived at that moment,
Carrying an empowering scent,
Spring gardens, full blossoms,
Filling the air with anticipation,
Messages seen and then hidden,
Flowers prevailing over sorrow,
That fear of losing her once more,
Tenderness and a serene day,
Conquering frosted losses,
Sprinkling my sky with blues and hues,
Gray setting up on some other shore,
Her presence brings harmony,
With one new day at a time,
Inspiring beauty, wandering gracefully,
Lost blooms, returning with memories,
Pushing aside desolate chills,
Arriving with blissful thoughts,
Breezing back into view.

THE CICADAS

Indulgent decibel depths, masked my thoughts,
Emerging cicada plagues, disguise loved eyes striking,
Conquering supple skin smiles, bordered locked hair,
Transporting your nectar soul, loved dearly,
Lost as I let you slide, tenderness unseen,
Fearing for a instant, deafened ears,
Itinerant insects overwhelm,
Cumbersome volume, on loves delicate mood,
I long for this air to be ours once more,
Locked from our thoughts,
Gaining fleeting freedom, emancipated wishes,
Never the owner of a caged bird, chosen soul,
Aching for our willing escape,
Unification at the humble table,
Filling my feasting heart once more,
Finding a silent shell,
Somewhere I can hear every word,
A loving exchange, an aggravated argument,
No meddling with bonded love,
Soon they will pass, into the garden ground,
Silent again, together in loves infatuation,
Drowned for minute,
Rapidly retaking the peace we crave.

THE PLAINS

Lost legions rest ahead, obeying the breeze,
Forever changing, anchored armies,
Displaying, parading, never advancing,
You are my floating abstraction,
Beyond a wooden race of ceremonial marchers,
As they sway like a Friday night bar,
Falling drunken, regrouping sober,
Never stirring your splendor,
Gliding upon a sovereign stream,
Standing tall over the spineless grasses,
Your colors light shift with expectation,
Uniforms swing from silver to gray,
Sun shadows, divided and whirling
Conquering my love,
Lifting me from the teeming mass,
Breaking free from earthly desires,
Fading blooms, the spoils of war,
Taking me into the consummate hills,
Together in lofty trees, leaving the raging battle,
Those pointless platoons on the plains.

THIS FACE BEFORE ME

Stirring next to the one I love,
She is soft as she sleeps,
Not a frown, visiting with a day of disappointment,
Drifting in a world, I cannot sense or embrace,
Materializing in this dream place,
A nightmare journal,
Joining her, floating with merciless memories,
Taking me along,
To fight a battle or castigate evil,
Holding her weary hand,
Wiping away ensuing tears,
It is tempting to wake her
but this could be that dream,
Where we walk hand in hand
bare foot upon clean sand,
Challenged only by an occasional extended wave,
Life mysteries and confrontation
hurled far out to sea,
Blown off course by a warm breeze,
Carrying new beginnings,
Refreshing air, hope and freedom,
As the salty sea corrodes the chains of the day,
Healing the wounds of existence,
Upon this face before me.

WE THREW IT ALL AWAY

Hurling our locked love, on that day in doubt,
Into the careless burly breeze,
Floating away with the pulled up surplus,
The nomadic litter of the land,
Disregarded with redundant wrappers,
Expired clipped transport tickets,
Desiccated leaves of a burnt summer,
Autumns up giving release,
Smaller bills, insignificant currency,
Seizing our chances at life apart,
Breaking downhill pieces, forgetting the whole,
Albums of severed snaps, massacred memories,
Unglued anticipation, absent pages,
Chapters chopped at will, now wanting,
Together in a rainbow stacked library,
Open freedom windows, an ocean draft,
Half of nothing, we threw it all away.

THE SPINNING ORB

We marched to the horizon boundary,
The sun still way out of reach,
Climbing the bitter stairs to the pole,
Discovering the stars, still way beyond,
Day tripping to the equatorial line,
The moon never chafing the surface,
Sailing into the distant thorny sea,
No edgy waterfall promise,
Scrambling high into endless night air,
The clouds offering no strength,
Sauntering towards the deepest south,
Not a ladder off the earth,
Creeping back to our humble haunt,
Taking her in my arms laughing.
Scaling the abrupt steps,
Finding a warm welcoming nest,
Making love until dawn,
Ignoring the spinning orb forever.

STALLED DRIFTWOOD

You walked the beach today,
Heading into the sinking sun,
Remembering you from before,
Looking toward the latest moon,
This time our eyes convening,
With a smile of renewed familiarity,
You glided past proud,
A dedicated voyage of an ocean liner,
As I bounced and stuttered
in the foaming boundary surf,
Enveloped in weeded remains
lifeless with the shells,
Enchanted by the oceanic tone,
Your sweetened perfume breeze,
Waiting on the ebbing shoreline,
For the tidal surge of your return,
Eager for you to select me
from amongst the scattered parts,
Disguised in shifting sands,
Pulled into the shingle depths,
Left misplaced, stalled driftwood in your wake.

NOWHERE TO GO

You were ready to leave today,
I would long for your smile,
Raging tempers and ghastly moods,
I know you would miss mine too,
Your muddled morning hair,
Fanatical adventures with a stubborn style,
An upturned bathroom,
Seeping sweet soapy air,
Seven outfit changes, slowing your exit,
At least a couple hours to talk you down,
From the teetering departure ledge,
Perfect makeup, accessories, a few minutes more,
Suicide relationships and everlasting love,
The neighbors eavesdropping,
Rather interesting, as they are not in love,
Divorce and bathroom activities, painless,
Then the start of a smile,
Slipping from my tightrope saunter,
Balancing scales requiring adjustment,
Maybe I could not believe, in life without you,
I am glad you had nowhere to go.

HOW MUCH DO I LOVE YOU?

How much do I love you? Never ask,
My feelings are not measured,
In pounds, ounces or grams,
No four-letter declaration, offered on a whim,

I never want to see, if I see you suffer,

I never want to feel, if I feel your pain,

I never want to hear, if I hear you sob,

I never want to taste, if life leaves you sour,

I never want my history, to be your future,

My soul runs in your veins, our blood is precious,
Your strength is my weakness,
Rights and ideals, my expectation,
In my arms, you are safe, but I am vulnerable,
Knowing one day I have to let you free,
In a world I know too well,
With little love and less understanding,
Always here for you, in body and spirit,
Love without charge or question,
Judgment, blame or reckoning,
A love everlasting, not quantifiable.

COMPLICATED NIGHTS

The night complicated everything,
By day I could see your eyes, study your mind,
Loving you, an open novel, with the living glow,
Not the silver of a leading light,
Alive too quickly and dying too soon,
Never aging until the next picture,
Having you walking at my side with the sun,
Solitary shadows joining, our long lonesome walks,
Growing taller as the day grows longer, so unlike life,
Bringing on a brisk evening,
Revealing the eyes of an early start,
Curves in the moonlit sands, furrowed shorelines,
Summoning night tripping travel,
Leaving me quiet, with no peace of mind,
As you float way from earth, running with the past,
Meeting doubtful demons and lost souls,
Childhood feuds, time lodged friends,
Revolting relatives, taking liberties with change,
Battling with the future until you rise,
Another day of sprinting hurdles,
Time to catch the sleep of an owl.

THE LAST CARAVAN

Dying embers lay sleeping,
The night nooks open,
Rising with you in my arms,
The beast tethered, another struggle,
Merging with corroded heaps,
Joining the careless cruisers,
Driven to the dock and nettles,
One handed reins, the other for yours,
Weighty loads rushing,
Crockery flustered, cutlery sharpened,
Scraping binding prevarications,
Dodging congested ditches.
Antagonizing snail, slower worm,
Taking life, one day at a time,
Generating an irate procession,
Turning on the flowing skeletal strip,
Fleeing winding high banks,
Bumping beside the planted avenue,
Counting fallen yearly rings, together,
Shuddering on murderous molehills,
Breaking ground with lichen bough,
Lifting for the closing day,
Searching for a tenant field,
Solitude with your soul,
Dry kindling for tonight.

THE CHAOTIC LOVE AFFAIR

Within the chaotic crowd of modest desert men,
I saw your dark pools, catching mine,
Emergent smiles and toyed hair,
Bunched keys and unlocked hearts,
Cutting a swath through the simple traders,
Penny market fruit and rolled carpet,
Lamplighters, extinguished, birdcages in flight,
Boxed dates, a rendezvous under canvas thoughts,
Medina and your hand in mine,
Away with the mules, the passing fennel camel carts,
Through the orange blossom dream fields,
Picking ladders and better luck,
Lively bees and rolling rosemary,
The scented Mediterranean mist,
Moisturizing full lips,
Wrecking sailor seas and forgotten fathers,
Landing with you,
Tears of departure, the final voyage,
Waving palms lining, the streets of occupation,
Morning coffee and your absent air.

ABSENCE

My world was plentiful; your departure left nothing,
I will never grow another garden rose,
Prospecting nurtured limbs in clay earth,
No first light chorus, raucous laughter,
Running streams, tripping water,
Steps and ladders, sunrise or sunset,
Committal dirges with mystified mourners,
Bright morning breezes and drinking water,
Reasons to wake,
Forgotten daybreak voices,
Humor bouncing, off a plain-faced wall,
The final drop discarded,
The wild urge to attain lightheaded heights,
Twenty-four hours lacking meaning,
I have already passed,
My lungs are sealed from anticipated air,
Hydration, a worthless act,
The nightmare remains, until I see you again,
Blood revisiting vacant veins,
Winded hair, folded in my arms,
Absence abandoned in your soft eyes.

I WONDER AT YOUR BEAUTY

I wonder at your beauty,
With years tripping near,
A minute since we first met,
Our souls calling,
One glance, you are in command,
A future shared, fleeting desire,
A modest nudge,
Empowering the earth, the two of us,
Walling all the inclement weather brings,
Renewed, fired and fueled each day,
Whether you dress to thrill or tried a little,
Make up like a model or not quite,
Hair styled to perfection,
Or morning hedge backwards,
It never matters much,
As you are the one I love,
Drawing me back, sharing,
Just the two of us.

EVERY TIME I RUFFLE YOUR FEATHERS

Every time I ruffle your feathers,
Stumbling and falling, into a quickly constructed hole,
Finding you at the foundation, in dismal darkness,
In haste I rush back to the surface,
Collapsing shingle walls, throwing sharp sand
into your dark smarting, suppurating eyes,
Scrambling again, you feel this blinding pain,
I lower my hand at attempted salvage,
Your reluctance, in abundance,
My futile efforts abandoned,
I must leave you now, in this darkness of my making,
Preparing for the cruel light of existence,
This time, my hand swathed in apology,
Coated with culpability,
Hopeful of departing reluctance,
Forgiveness forthcoming,
Your feathers rested, eyes clear bright,
As I offer you the world,
In part exchange for your smile.

YOUR TEARS

Looking into your nomadic eyes,
Witnessing welling tears,
Soon stridently flowing, mountain falls,
Sorrow overwhelming your facade,
A changing landscape, profound rain,
Valleys usually bearing your radiant smile,
Awash with tinted brackish streams,
Drawing more from nimbus clouds
Muddying a once sapphire sky,
An overcast perspective,
Merging and hiding crystal clarity,
The downpour continuing unhindered,
My words are too gentle to be heard,
Arms unable to dam this torrential flow,
I will spend the day, pleading for a pause,
A handkerchief courier,
Searching for your warming sun.

SECRETED IN TIME

I want to delight in this moment forever,
Taking those russet eyes to safety,
In an ugly world,
Hold out my hands and push away the harm,
Pluck you from the earth,
Fold you carefully within a time proof blanket,
Coat your precious skin,
With age defying ointments from distant lands,
Shelter you from the cruel elements,
Take you out on only the clearest days,
Breathing the fresh and clean air,
Whilst harsh rays and hate are sleeping,
Box you warily for war; release you only in peace,
Slide you into some secret place,
When strife strolls across the barren land,
Release you into a new era of hope,
When natural beauty has been forgotten.

HURRIED DEPARTURE

You are leaving with an overnight bag,
Smaller than our first date,
You will need more than a simple suitcase or two,
There is no space, for my heartache and pain,
No room for pleasure or contentment,
Nothing large enough, for the love we shared,
No filing room for those records and years of tickets,
No place for a multitude of smiles,
A container for tears,
A special compartment, for our letters and thoughts,
Nothing large enough for the journeys we fulfilled,
No light to shed, upon the darkness of today,
No comfortable nest, for our growing child,
A pocket for the bond that held us together,
Space for the freedom that sets us apart.

THE ETERNAL MIST

Passing into my arms, riding the frozen dewy dawn,
The shrouding haze, tenderness cloaked,
This consuming apparition of emerging beauty,
A day of dearth, no longer possible,
Now addicted to a daily search of gray-fogged trees,
Quickly we grew together,
Wading the watered woodland of dreams,
The leafy canopy peering down
upon my static weakness,
An effortless objective, for a merciless axe man,
Thrown together fragile, optimistic and faithful,
Fleeting stability gifted, an undying vision,
Possession would lead to destruction,
Happiness departed with your need to grow,
I remained rooted in this revelation of you,
Lost for a while in distant condensed air,
Your arrival burning away my wintry desolation,
Traveling upon the smoldering daybreak sun,
Once again, living with your captivating spell,
An evergreen anticipation of the eternal mist.

HOPE AND WONDER

Advancing on a freshly mowed sky,
Corresponding with clouds and a confident future,
Soon shattered, this heaven hung pane,
A thousand pieces grounded glistening,
On a parched earthen road, scratched through oblivion,
Penetrating pastures, for greener grass,
Again disappointed, a different color, same old fence,
Throwing up infinite insecure sand,
Holding her in my arms, a protecting father,
A foolish man, carrying childhood dreams,
On an expedition, without expectation,
Joining this human fallacy,
Head to head again, some new confrontation,
The featured ideology of the week,
Sitting tagged in the bargain basement window,
Some redundant promise, piled high, sold cheap,
The latest pompous philosophy, power hungry fools,
Offer your own sacrifices this time,
Count us absent, when drawing your flawed plans,
I am holding her tight for as long as I can,
Hold me liable, in contempt,
Drag me to the highest court, on earth at least,
She is mine, sheltered with life and soul,
You cannot extinguish the burning sun,
Torching your scorched earth promise,
The moon will heal the lesions of the day,
Soon you will be gone, dropped slowly,
Into some hallowed opening,
Swathed with hope and wonder,
Food for maggots and mother earth.

A COLD SUMMER DAY

She left me in the waterless dust,
On a frozen day in June,
Never knowing the chill of summer, until then,
Solstice moments, endless waking,
Sour sunrays and stationary earth,
The pain of dawn, noontime on ice,
Into the depths of a disastrous dusk,
Eternal night, absent affection,
Stopping for falling auburn leaves,
The hearth fires of winter weeks,
Longing for the showers of April,
To clear my suffering heart.

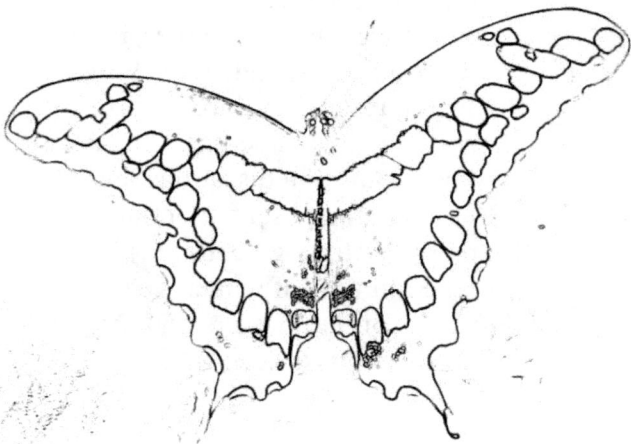

THE BUTTERFLY

Rising with the daybreak sun,
Growing in the early hours, life had just begun,
Morning dew, changing form,
Independence handed you wings,
A novice alone in the midday glare,
Powerful basking rays for an instant,
Burning and growing,
Experience moving you on,
Afternoon achievements, surfacing prospects,
A partner in pursuit, you created more,
Breaking as the sun bathed the west, a fleeting siesta,
Your brilliance starting to fade
with mountain scraping rays,
Falling below the heady horizon trail,
A day of seasons, minutes for a while,
The sprouting sanguine spring,
A playful idle summer,
Spinning sliding colors, autumn's guarantee,
Thoughts of a weary winter, a day upon the wing,
The light slipping to another world of dawn,
Peace descending,
Joining the apprehension of nightfall,
Accepting the silence of everlasting sleep,
A new moon lifted you into the wintry sky,
Earth would never overlook,
The joy of your the vibrant array.

INTO THE LIGHT

Squinting into the knothole of daylight,
From the gloomy shell of my conception,
This place where I exist and never flourish,
Cloistered short-lived days,
An obscure land, without liberty,
Banishing attempted dialogue,
Meetings and acknowledgements cancelled,
Merely visitors passing by, nothing more,
I see the wall-dancing silhouette of your love,
Only your radiance can break this barricade,
Alluring and dissolving away my refuge,
Open to your loving advance,
Shedding me from the shadows forever.

IN A HEATED MOMENT

In a heated moment,
My words score deep,
Even though I ruffle and graze,
I sit once more, hurting too,
Your absence aches more,
Now I am lost, alone once more,
With isolated thoughts, simple regrets,
So much has passed us by,
I still have space in my heart,
Room by my side,
There is more to be done,
Further journeys, distant lands,
No voyage is complete without you,
My love never travels alone,
From now on, I will tether my tongue,
Only to be released,
When expressing my love for you.

STRONGER EACH DAY

The flowers I gave you, on our first date,
Have wilted into yesterdays dust,
Growing with old news,
The car I drove,
Driving days over, twisted into something new,
Washing whites,
The chocolate I offered you,
Melted in the sun soaked recycled dashboard
of that same car,
The meal we ate,
Tasteless and well past its sell by date,
The clothes we wore,
Out of vogue for a moment,
Returning last week for another run,
The shoes we sported,
Worn out miles ago,
On a thousand pavement adventures,
The smiles we exchanged,
Still here for each other,
Despite a miserable world of change,
The commitment we shared,
Enduring the trials of time, the jealously of people,
The love I gave you,
Has grown stronger each day,
An established tree on a perfect horizon.

YOUR RETURN

I was only a child, but I felt the meaning,
Your gesture thrust upon me,
Looking into my eyes and handing me a branch,
Olives of peace, with strength and a smile,
I saw the fire, starting with a glimmering flame,
Tenderness holding, twisting my heart
Pastry in the hands of a master chef,
Memories carved in the bark of my soul,
Then you were gone,
My solitary representative of forbidden love,
No pressures of caste and culture,
Holding hands, a momentary union,
The colors at the surface, so different
The blood within, unity shared by humankind,
Then you were lost,
Your sparkling eyes haunted my soul, never forgotten,
One day I hoped to witness your return,
I longed, as time passed by
never fading, the search continued,
Procrastination slowed the rapidity,
Clouding my judgment, leaving me gazing into space,
Possessed by world-weariness,
Then into this contemplation you arrived,
Illuminating the heavy shadow of loss,
Banishing confusion with simplicity,
Your intoxicating smile,
Your supple lips satisfying my heart,
Those eyes framed in locks of hair, enduring beauty,
Filling my world with your return.

THE MISTRESS OF DECEPTION

Deceiving succulent greens, enticed me unaware,
Distracting colors crowned, camouflaged expectation,
Swindled extravagance, your effervescent palette,
Organized stockpiles of piercing people,
Set for an effortless kill,
Ready to consume fresh warm juice,
Served at ninety-eight point six,
Escape is useless, scheming sinewy arms
accommodate strangulation,
The rustling invigorating breeze, natures release,
Soon drowned by your echoing mirth,
Commanding a sliding legless cavalry, poison ready,
Flanked by eight footed couriers,
Ensnaring glued nets, trapping readiness,
Salivating daggers primed,
Under the cruel heels of a deceptive mistress.

THE PORT

She sailed towards me, through beleaguered water,
A blade through softness,
Freshly sharpened, easily dividing,
Billowing cloth extended,
As I lay ahead, a coracle in her corridor,
Sleek lines and straining figurehead,
Running for my modest home,
She was without obstacle until now,
Joining the cowering flotsam,
Sheltering her from tempestuous odds,
For a while we are together,
Safe among the decked silk,
Soon her sails would grasp a clement breeze,
Heading for uncharted streams alone,
Voyaging out of sight, never out of mind,
Leaving me behind, longing for another storm.

RUSTED HEARTS

You left me floating with cold rusted hearts,
On a broken saddened sea,
Drifting in the walled apathetic breeze,
Forgotten forsaken wandering souls,
Spilling from a splintered core,
Soured and pleading for fluid honey,
Running with cruelly severed veins,
Searching for sticking tape solutions,
Tortured spirit shelves,
Cautiously labeled, life expectations,
Tender treachery, monotonous monogamy,
Planed and square fenced floors,
Bottled green grass promises,
Coined questions, suited legal people,
Tangled reefs with rotten wrecks,
The outdated model, next month's plot,
You left me floating with the cold rusted hearts.

VEILED MYSTERY

Netted softness concealing the face I love,
Placing her in mystifying light,
Gazing into shrouded features,
Searching for a welcoming smile,
Finding dark forest ponds,
Beauty in a rain spell suffused woodland,
Mesmerized by naked orb web curtains,
Sprouting buds, a new acquaintance,
Expressions of clandestine obscurity,
Soon discovering, a new purpose,
Fuelling my imagination, firing devotion,
A futile filmy disguise,
Holding on to hidden bracken paths,
The engine of our romance,
Future findings, enduring expeditions,
Continuing to discover,
Never deciphering natures code,
Keeping love alive in a wasteland breeze,
Feeding and watering my allotted garden,
Focusing upon, an undying love.

THE ROWDY GULLS

Just two seafarers, upon uncharted water,
Searching for surfacing rocks,
Everything stalking sustenance,
Starting such a promising voyage,
New land hopes, abundant treasures,
The rowdy gulls mocking us from the outset,
Oblivious fish, flirting currents beneath,
Sailing into unknown streams,
Deep green and mysterious,
You stared above and I gazed ahead,
Others scoffed as we entered the open sea,
Joined each day by sun and haze,
Through bitter storms, wall like waves,
Those moments when only survival mattered,
Holding tight when our dreams went overboard,
Together prevailing against those odds,
Where were those gulls?

WOODEN TULIPS

I never remembered which way to turn,
Leaving the parallel station,
There was a bridge and water,
In every direction,
Six stories and living barges,
Curtains over canals,
All I seemed to recall, was your parting words,
Bring me home some tulips,
I thought about those colored cups all day,
Close to a few cycling calamities en route,
Here for a moment and wilted in a few,
I found a carver with devoted hands,
Woodworking miles away,
From the regimented rows,
Tinted iconic fields,
Endless dream mills,
Tattered sails and level canvas,
Here are your symbolic blooms,
Carved and painted well,
My love for you will always last,
So why not your flowers too.

FOR SHE IS GONE

Lost, looking into this blackened void before me,
Everything said, water washed away,
Words piped up into the ether breeze,
Commingling with others out there,
Good, ghastly and gone regardless,
Those worthless annotations,
Words out of order,
Not syllables for infant education,
Crushed, solitary shattered script,
Painful pieces of a valuable volume,
Glancing towards the papered trees,
I can only wish, they had never been felled,
Pulp for every etched card, my folded letters,
The fluid ink for this instrument of emotional release,
Never invented,
Spoken words not enough, to transmit true sentiment,
Setting this pointless instrument to toil,
Listing decisive feelings, trust and love for you,
Only time preventing, a work in stone or steel,
Still, the message would have strayed,
Eroded or rusted back to the floor,
Unlit eyes failing, sculpted ears boarded,
You are gone.

THE PHOTOGRAPH

I had ensnared this figure of beauty,
A passing guiding light,
Color, the last thing on my mind,
Seeing those contour shadows,
Beauty in deep dark pools of desire,
An infinite well of mystery, open to endless discovery,
Lips of likelihood, thirsty full and yearning,
Boundless love, overtly sensual,
Tripping with potential,
Soft rolling hills in a fascinating landscape,
A proud chin carrying it to the heavens,
Enjoying you from all angles and fields of view,
Imagining your face next to mine,
Knitted enduring kisses,
The sweetness of your smile
disguising a passionate woman,
Awakened by running hands,
Through your dark and coiling hair,
Feeling your mind
smoothing upon your neck, taking strength,
Holding your confident head high in adversity,
I longed for you to leap into my arms once more.

THE MELANCHOLY RUCKSACK

I hauled my melancholy rucksack through life,
Pen, paper, camera and a lens or two,
Often catching precious moments,
Advancing on my scratchy pen,
Developing life, anticipation of the early hours,
Printing splendor at eleven by fourteen,
Inscribed losses too tender to frame,
Every time our union grazed its knees, you cried twice,
I glued our devotion back together with ink and essay,
You asked me to stop, sad verse made you sob,
I ceased writing about love,
Instead, plucking on the straws of existence,
Discovering reason and sporadic optimism,
Frequently drawing short, occasionally long,
You whispered how you missed my poems,
The notion made me beam,
Again, I picked up my inky marker,
Sometimes you smiled, but seldom wept,
Never again did you ask me to stop.

THE FLOWER GARDEN

You are my flower,
In a garden of engaging blooms,
Each with a matchless perfume,
Climbing and standing,
Rolling edges and cascading rockeries,
Bedded bulbs, hectic heathers,
Spring tulips and proud lilies,
Inspected daily,
Rinsing away the arrogant aphids,
Flighty butterflies and greedy birds
Taking stock with toiling bees,
I am just the humble gardener,
Tending to every need,
Watering, feeding and nurturing,
Clearing wearisome weeds,
Picking you up after a stimulating storm,
Hiding you from frozen fingers,
Desiring only fragrant pollen,
Your sweet nectar and abundant seeds.

ABOUT THE AUTHOR

Nicholas Price is a poet whose work has been published through a series of bespoke and mainstream publications and books.

With a legacy of work now collated and published in several new titles, bringing a unique poetic style and perspective to a wide range of subjects enjoyed by all readers and ages.

His poetry, writings and photographic work have been exhibited at key events and institutions. The acclaimed collection titled *Cleared Hot!* – a photographic story and essay - was acquired by one of the world's most prestigious institutions, the United States Library of Congress.

OTHER AVAILABLE TITLES

BRIDGES TO MANHATTAN
and other poetic journeys

Nicholas A. Price

America is a way of life and a state of mind, to be savored and discovered.
Nicholas Price celebrates this beauty and diversity through his poetic artistry. His journeys take us from the Bridges to Manhattan to the pioneer trails of the West Coast and beyond.

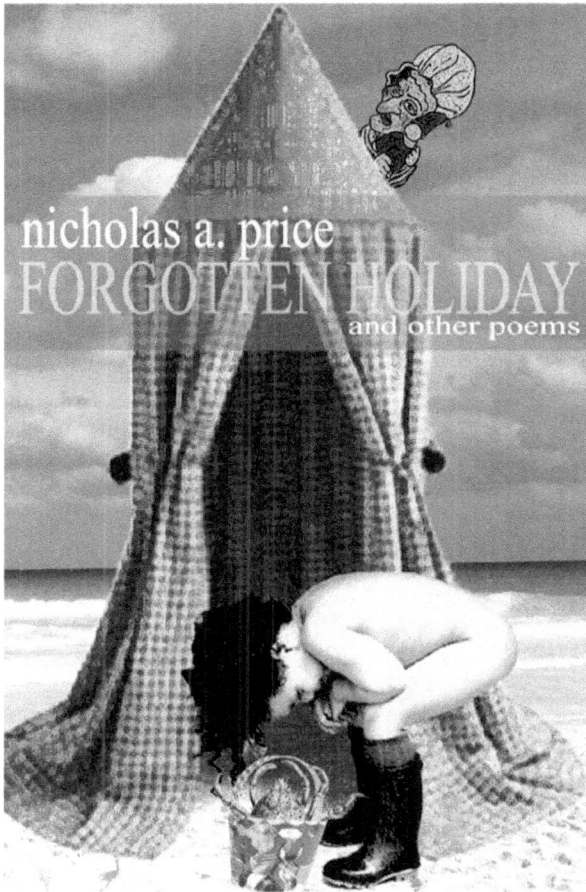

nicholas a. price
FORGOTTEN HOLIDAY
and other poems

Nicholas Price takes us on a poetic journey through childhood and life experience.
Nostalgic, amusing and a must read for those who sometimes question; "whatever happened to the world we grew up in?"

Forgotten Holiday is one book to keep amongst your own treasure trove of memories.

an ELEPHANT
IN MY FRONT YARD
and other observations

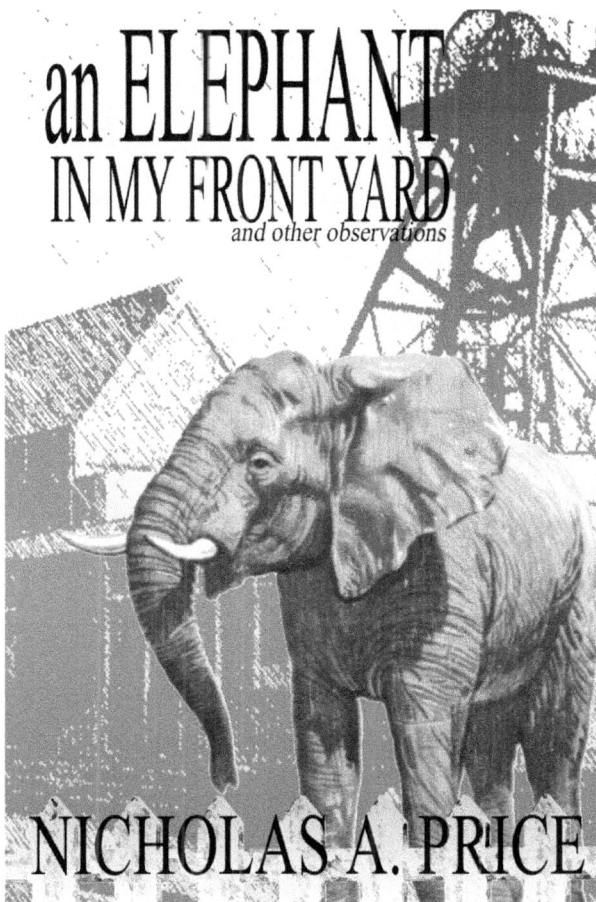

NICHOLAS A. PRICE

Nicholas Price presents his frank and sometimes humorous poetic
thoughts and observations on life.
From social and political change to the hopes of us all.

Described as "a refreshing new voice in poetry", these works are
timeless and reflective of the world we once knew and the one we
have become.

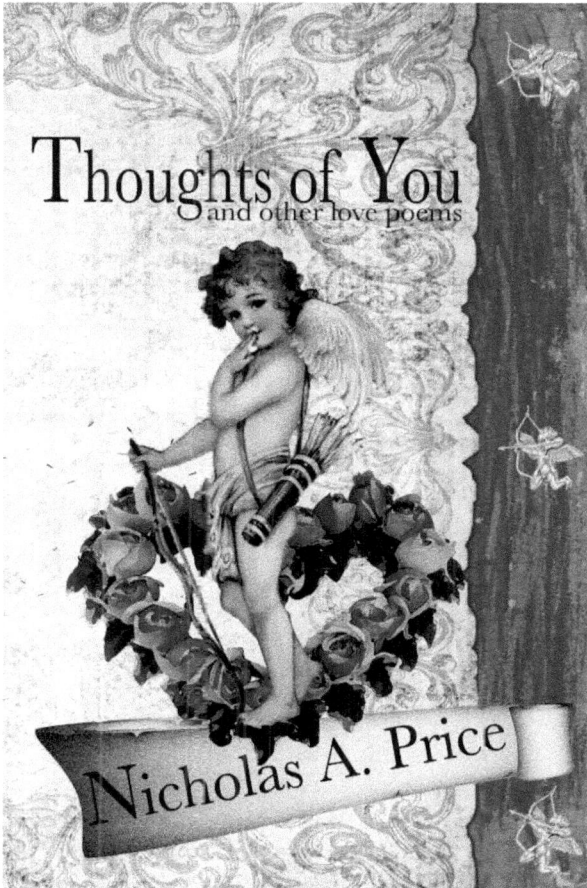

Thoughts of You
and other love poems

Nicholas A. Price

How would you describe being in love to someone who has never experienced it?
Poet Nicholas Price pens the human storms of desire, heartbreak and devotion.
The distant yearning to unyielding passion, absence and infidelity, grief and solitude, those erratic and chaotic emotions we call love.

Tough Tribe
ToughTribe.com

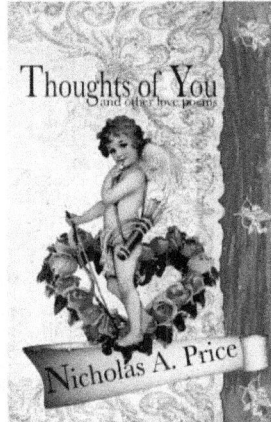

Buy All Four Books At Our Special
Collector Set Price

www.ToughTribe.com
Also available at Amazon.com and all other fine bookstores

www.ingramcontent.com/pod-product-compliance
Lightning Source LLC
LaVergne TN
LVHW021358080426
835508LV00020B/2345